MANNERS IN THE GREAT KINGDOM

MANNERS IN THE GREAT KINGDOM

© 2021 SEZ GIN

Design: H&D

Illustration: H&D

Publishing and Printing: Tredition GmbH, Hlenreie 40-44, 22359 Hamburg

ISBN 978-3-347-30258-7 | Paperback

ISBN 978-3-347-28868-3 | Hardcover

ISBN 978-3-347-30259-4 | E-Books

ISBN: 4067248367544   I Audiobook

CONTENT

The lack of knowledge and laziness are the biggest enemies

 "Max, sit down and listen carefully to what I will tell you. Now you are seventeen years old, and you are crown prince. Till now, we have been teaching you many things with teachers from our kingdom, and all that you know is a theory; you have to understand some truths outside the kingdom. You must spend at least a year traveling to other kingdoms to observe how people live, understand the challenges they face and the consequences of their actions, and experience all of this. You have to get wiser in order to rule our kingdom. You will get wiser when you get more knowledge. The question is how accurately you will evaluate the knowledge you acquire about morals and values. Good manners are the basis of excellent health and a successful life. The man is complete when he/she has spiritual, mental, and physical health. We have no doubts that we educated you for a crown prince. Our best teachers were teaching you. You can cope with all subjects, including sports. You have been living only in the castle, and you know only one side of the coin. It is essential to see the other side of the coin—how other people live. However, our kingdom is highly respected.

How did you know that hundreds of years ago, your grandparents worked tirelessly, engaged in negotiations, displayed patience, and demonstrated selflessness to maintain the balance of all kingdoms? A one-kilometer area, bordered by the borders of the other kingdoms, serves as a free trading zone, allowing all traders to travel there and engage in trade with each other. This boundary is impenetrable, ensuring our safety from all threats. Moreover, we have four buildings on our side that serve as entrances to the free trading zone. Both of the buildings serve as courts. Kingdoms designate one building for resolving disputes and looting, while the other serves as a platform for arbitrage. To be more precise, we are the ones conducting the arbitrage. The other building houses the major traders who engage in cross-kingdom trade. The other two buildings are keeping money safe. Other kings can use one of them to safeguard their treasures, as it contains keys and rooms for each. We reserve the final building for the bid traders. We only keep them safe. Everyone is aware of their immense reserves, which is why they refrain from attacking us, fearing that their actions would incite others' anger. Our grandparents have done everything, and it is our duty to uphold and rebuild these laws. This explains why we possess the largest library. It is our most powerful weapon. We gather all stories and lessons for future reference. We know that knowledge is more powerful than every weapon. With speech control, you can conquer everyone by controlling their feelings.

At your age, young people travel to other kingdoms and share information with us about their superior manufacturing capabilities, the news they have learned, the quality of their kings' rule, the taxes they have imposed, and their intentions. We require this information because it aids us in our interactions with kings and traders. When we comprehend new developments, we implement them in our kingdom to enhance the quality of life for our people. Moreover, we identify the areas with the best harvests, purchase them from them, and then sell them to other kingdoms at a profit. For instance, once we determine which village is selling the best wagons, we purchase them, travel to the free zone, and then sell them to other kingdoms. When an individual possesses knowledge, they are free from the fear of failure. To possess good knowledge, one must possess good manners, cultivate good habits, exercise control over their emotions, and adhere to all other factors that contribute to mental clarity. We take care of every person in our kingdom, and we are kind and respectful to people from other kingdoms; that is why they respect us. It's time to travel to other kingdoms to gain knowledge and implement what you see as beneficial and new in our kingdom. My advice is to describe everything that you think is good, and when you meet a wise person, visit her or him; that is very important for you. Those people are an unlimited source of knowledge. We maintain good health, love, and amity with both close and unknown people.

We derive our knowledge from the good manners and habits we employ daily to navigate all situations without causing harm to anyone. For us, it is important to help everyone and everything. Not only must we be fair, but we also need to understand the situation correctly. To know the actual situation, we have to know the situation on all sides of the coin in order to judge the way that, even if convicted, to be satisfied. The Lord has created us in a way that allows us to injure ourselves while simultaneously fostering the development of our personalities, enabling us to leave a lasting legacy that is both meaningful and beautiful. In order to have balance, there will always be good and bad, black and white, and smiles and tears. The man lives with his/her body, mind, and soul. The Lord has created us in such a way that only two bodies, minds, and two souls can create the new life of the new soul with a new body and a new mind. To remain in our human bodies, we require numerous allowances from healthy, thinking individuals who maintain balance and harmony. However, this can only be achieved with knowledge. Being born into a good family and achieving success is not enough; you need support to develop into a person with strong character and good manners, not just for the physical body but also for the soul and mind, for inner peace. That's why, son, tomorrow, dress like a normal person, grab your inkpot and quill, and write everything that's important to you. This will enhance your wisdom and make you wiser and fairer.

With your writings, you will leave the knowledge to the new generation, and you will show them the mistakes that they should not make again. I wish you success in your journey and good luck on your comeback at eighteen years old. Let the Lord keep you safe."

A person always has a choice

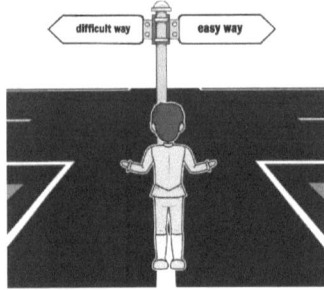 Max woke up. After eating his breakfast and bidding farewell to his mother, father, and sister, Max went to his teacher, who had prepared all the necessary items for his journey. He must remember to pack clothes, a bag, and instructions in case anything unexpected arises during his journey. Max carefully put on his clothes, listened to his teacher's recommendations, and proceeded to the other kingdoms. In the middle of the day, a car stopped next to Max. In that car were a well-dressed father and a son. The father was in his 40s, and his son was twenty years old. The car was brimming with fruits and vegetables.

"Hi! Where are you going, son?" asked the driver.

"I am going to the next kingdom," said Max.

"We are also going there. Come in the car; we will leave you there."

"I order to start a conversation, Max," said the father.

"For how many days will you sell the goods?" asked Max.

"The products are not for sale; they are for exchange." Answer the father and continue to speak.

"In our kingdom, it's clear that people have been living in this manner for many years. All the peasants are obligated to live that way in order to get fewer illnesses. Maintaining good hygiene not only prolongs our lives but also enhances our appearance. It is time for my son to get married, but he is still searching for a bride from our kingdom, and we are going to search for her in another kingdom. However, in order to choose a bride, we need to find a girl who is clean and hardworking enough to live in our kingdom. For many years, it has been a custom that, when a boy and a girl don't get along, we select a girl from a different kingdom based on our mutual preferences. In reality, we trade fruits and vegetables from home, where there are girls ready for marriage, for garbage. We ask people from villages with marriage-ready girls to stop there. In the house where there is less garbage and our son likes her, we will ask her for a wife. When we say that we are from the great kingdom, the parents always agree because they know that the life there is better, and we live with love and commitment.

"You've discovered an excellent solution for boys, but I'm confident that there are girls in the great kingdom who face similar issues. How you are deciding such problems?" said Max.

"We have also found a solution to that problem. We took this into consideration when we created the rules for the great kingdom. Every two years we are organizing a race for boys from other kingdoms who are ready for marriage. We determine places where new houses have to be built, having in mind the number of girls who have to be married. The race is based on who is better at his

job: masons, smiths, tailors, carpenters, and boys with many other abilities. At the same time in the race, they are building houses for the new families. The masons are putting brigs; the carpenters are making tables, chairs, fences, and beds needed for the new houses. The tailors are stitching all the necessary items for the houses. Our king sources all the materials directly. Therefore, the new family has a solid foundation for life, experiencing fewer problems and greater family happiness. The girls and their families make up the jury, observing the working process closely. When they like a boy, they send the girl to help and encourage him. If the boy likes the girl, he will allow her to come and help him. This helps them meet, marry, and find a home."

Two other roads split off from the main road. "I wish you good luck and success; I will take the other road."

"I wish you the same for you young boy, and continue driving the cart."

Strive to work on what brings you pleasure

 Max was walking along the road in the forest when a man approached him. He was moving so quickly that it appeared as though he was in a hurry to reach his destination.

"Hello, traveler, where are you going so fast?" asked Max.

"Hello, young boy! I am going to the next kingdom. There is one very wise man from whom I am planning to get advice. If you agree, we can begin our journey together, during which I will share my personal story with you. My name is Nobel."

Max has nothing against hearing his story, and he was delighted to hear it. As they walked slowly, Nobel began to share his story with Max.

"When I was a small boy, we never had much money in my family. My mother would often remark that she had never married a man who, through his craft, earned a substantial income to support his family's daily needs. Every time I wanted her to buy me something, she always told me that she did not have money, and that is why when I grow up, I want to learn a craft that is profitable so my kids will not suffer like

15

me. At the age of eighteen, I heard a story about a man in a distant kingdom who possessed extensive knowledge about large predators. I believed that if he was well-versed in large predators, he could impart his knowledge to me, enabling me to become a proficient predator. Only a select few can master this skill and not fear these creatures. Those who fear these creatures will generously donate large sums of money to ensure their safety from these predators. That's why I took all the money from my parents, began my search for him, and eventually found him. When I found him, I asked him, "Please, teacher, teach me how to kill giant predators!"

"It is not so easy. You need many years to learn the skills necessary to defeat them. Are you prepared to spend the next few years with me in that forest? Are you prepared to listen and learn continuously from morning to evening? We will solely focus on theoretical knowledge, as there aren't any large creatures present here," responded the teacher.

"I am prepared to undertake all necessary tasks!" I answered him without getting deeper into his words.

"Do you have enough money to pay me for the education? I need to have a source of income to support myself while I'm teaching you."

"I'll pay you everything to learn how to defeat those predators." I spoke confidently, envisioning the greatness I would achieve.

He accepted and allowed me to live with him. Two years have passed. I was following the instructions of my skilled teacher with outstanding care and attention. I was listening to him very carefully and gave all my energy to learn everything he wanted me to. He instructed me on how to construct traps and various other strategies for capturing a large creature. At the end, the teacher told me, "Now you know everything that I know. Now you can defeat every predator that you see."

I left satisfied, even if I had no money. I was thrilled that I could now kill large creatures; I was well-versed in dinosaurs, mammoths, and other mythical creatures. I was among the few who possessed this knowledge. I was proudly walking to the cities and villages, offering my services to people.

"What are you capable of doing, young boy?" they inquired.

"I am capable of eliminating large predators to protect you from them!" I was bragging.

"Oh, alright! When those creatures appear, we will certainly call you, but for now, we do not need your services."

"That was how the days, months, and years of my life unfolded. People did not hire me, but I also did not hear that those creatures appeared. Most likely, their disappearance occurred many years ago. I am unable to work and am currently living a life filled with misery and poverty. Therefore, I am turning to the wise man for guidance. I hope that he will help me. "

We arrived on the hill where the wise man's house stood in the evening. The wise man welcomed us, provided us with food, and provided us with a shelter for the night. He assured us that he would answer our questions when we woke up in the morning. However, he reminded us that the day is wiser than the night because it allows our body and mind to rest, which allows him to provide more accurate answers. We woke up, and we saw that on the table there was food. The wise man instructed us to wash our heads and hands in the river, eat breakfast, and then return to him. We followed the old man's instructions and sat down next to him.

"I am listening to you," the old man said, and Nobel began to narrate his story once more, this time to the old man.

The wise man remained silent for a moment before launching into his speech: "Education ignites a fire; it does not imply filling the vessel. Your environment forces you to seek something that will help you progress. Many people follow this path, but in your situation, you confront large predators that have disappeared over time, requiring a slight shift in your perspective and mindset. You can take on the role of a shepherd and occasionally engage in combat with small predators or even a bear. Once upon a time, there was a mighty man whose name was Buddha.

When asked how to find his calling in front of them, he replied, "Imagine waking up with all the wealth in the world and still wanting to do something else to make you happy and loved." This is what you should strive for, as engaging in activities filled with love prevents boredom. When you enjoy something, it's likely that others will find it enjoyable as well. You must understand that people value excellent skills that are beneficial to them, and they are willing to pay for them. If the desire for money didn't blind you, you wouldn't seek out that teacher; instead, you would seek out a different teacher who could impart knowledge from your heart. A person learns while they are still alive. When you were a young boy, it's likely that you had a dream, or perhaps while you were walking around your village, you saw a craftsman at work, and you wished to emulate him. Life continues, and you must strive to achieve your goals. Remember, you will leave behind whatever you build or do, but the choice is yours. I cannot dictate what you should work on; you must consider your options and make your own decisions." The old man stood up and said that he had something to do.

"Thank you for your hospitality and for your advice for Nobel. I am confident that we will discuss this matter, and he will make a decision. I wish you to be healthy." Max left some coins for the old man and walked away. While others were going about their lives, Nobel remained in silence.

If there is hope, there will always be a future

Max had been walking for two days when he finally spotted someone. In the evening, in the middle of the field, he saw a young man who was sitting on the ground and was crying. In front of him there was a pile of coals. He went next to him and set down.

"Hello! What happened? Why do you look so sad?"

The young man erased his tears and answered, "My name is Tom. I will share my experience of sadness with you. Yesterday, during my travels, I came across a small tree amidst the untamed wilderness. I sat next to it, and I decided to rest, and I thought, "How small it is, even if that makes me shadow. I snuggled under its crown and slept peacefully. After an hour, I woke up and felt that my stomach was gurgling from hunger. Then, I noticed that there were fruits hanging from the branches. I plucked them and ate them. The evening came, and it got colder. I didn't have any warm clothes on and felt trapped, so I decided to start a fire to avoid freezing in the evening. I quickly built a small tree out of matchwood, burning it to a high temperature before going to sleep. I woke up the next morning. The sun was shining brightly, and my stomach was once again rumbling with hunger. However, the tree that had shielded me from the sun and provided me with food was no longer there. At that moment, I came to understand the consequences of my actions. I had to reflect on the ways in which the shadow had aided me and provided me with delicious fruits. I had to understand that every next person who found him would also help that person, so I destroyed it. How reckless I was. A person who lacks self-control and acts solely to satisfy their own needs harms others."

Max took a brad from its bag and two pieces of dried meat; he gave him the half of it. He also had an extra shirt, which he gifted to the young man as a present. After they finished their meal, he told the young man, "While you cannot change the past, you can focus on the future. When you realized the mistake, you took a huge step ahead. Therefore, you have the right to fight. Try to achieve something important for you that will be beneficial for others. Make a goal and work on achieving it. Once you reach your goal, you will plant numerous trees and be able to assist others who are similar to you. I will tell you one parable; you make your own conclusions.

They were quietly and calmly lighting three candles in a room.

All their conversations, even the cracking of their flames, were audible in the silence. "I am peace," said the first one. "Regrettably, individuals are unable to rescue me. They cannot save me. They are incapable of valuing me, nor do they strive for my well-being. I believe they have nothing left for me, and I must let go. It just motioned, and it lit out.

The second candle says, "My name is Faith. However, it appears that my presence is also unnecessary. People seem disinterested in my presence. That is why there is no point to burn, and it also lighted out.

The third one said sadly, "I am Love, but I do not have strength to burn more. People avoid me, and they tend to forget me. They lack the ability to both give and receive love." The third candle also lighted out.

At this moment, a child entered the room. Upon noticing that three candles remained unlit, the child began to yell. "But what are you doing? Why are you not lighting up? I'm afraid of the dark."

The fourth candle, whose flame glowed in the darkness, began to speak in a nervous tone, "Do not be afraid. Do not cry. Until I ignite, you have the opportunity to illuminate other candles. I am hope. Until hope exists, there will always be a future. Now, go to sleep knowing that tomorrow we will continue with the hope for your future.

There is nothing more valuable than health

 It was a wonderful day. He was walking along the road near the village, which was next to a lake. He spotted four men carrying a stretcher nearby. He hurried up to catch them. Max noticed that four robust men were carrying a wealthy but elderly man on a richly decorated stretcher. Max welcomed them and started walking with them. A few meters away from them, a poor cabin was occupied by a man who was talking loudly.

"Ah, I wonder when I will endure such suffering. The world is black for me. Should I kill myself?"

Obviously, the old man heard the sighs and complaints of the young man, and he ordered the servants to stop. The old man asked, "Why are you so desperate?"

"Ah, sir, how can't I be desperate?" answered the young man. "How not be sad when I am very poor? I am willing to sacrifice everything to achieve the same level of wealth as you. I will live a lavish lifestyle, and I will glorify the Lord's generosity. Now, I am working all day for only one piece of bread and a handful of olives. Is that a life?

"Why are you complaining? "Answered the old man. You are richer than me.

"How can I be richer than you?" The young man stared, wondering. "Look, sir, my purse is always empty, my legs are too tired to hold me, my hands cannot hold anything, and my eyes are always watching like a hungry wolf," he said.

"Let me cut your tired legs, and I will pay you for them one thousand golden coins," said the old man.

"What?" Screamed the young man. Even if you give me ten times one thousand golden coins, I will not give them to you.

"Fine. Sell me your empty hands, and I will pay you in gold as much as they weigh."

"Even if you overwhelm me with money, I will not give them."

"Fine! Sell me your hungry eyes. I will reward you with one hundred purses filled with golden coins, and I will also gift you with my castle and garden."

"What are you saying, sir? To get blind? I refuse to give up my eyes, regardless of the wealth on Earth," the young man responded.

"Eh, boy!" said the old man. "Now can you see that you are richer than me? You are young, strong, and healthy; there is no greater wealth than that. I am old and ill. Even if I give all my treasures, I cannot buy even one day's health and youth. Do not complain, do not anger the Lord; he is generous to you! For instance, when I was younger, I aspired to wealth, gold, land, and power, and I worked diligently to achieve these goals. I held everyone in high regard, which led to a lack of time for my family, relatives, friends, and dependents. Being wealthy is not a negative thing, but we also need to make time for our mental well-being, our souls, and the small, priceless things in life. But I realized it too late. Before three days had passed, I was dreaming that death would be my fate. It gives me a few days before that to prepare, and then it will take me. It gives me that right because when I was working or willing wealth, land, and gold, I was feeding many; I did not hear other people, and I had put many efforts to do that. I offered all my wealth for more time to enjoy life, but it reduced me. I am now embarking on a journey to revisit my childhood favorite place. Before I go. What I've come to understand, young man, is that we must set aside time for our favorite activities. However, we often forget it when we are living our lives. One thing is certain: time is the most valuable asset we possess, and we should not allow it to be lost. That's why you need to stop complaining, take control of your life, and use the time you have for happiness, your favorite people, work, wealth, and beneficial things that can make other people happy. Remember, the most important thing is how other people will remember you." He placed a few coins on the ground before leaving.

"I may not require them, but they can instill courage in you. I wish you to be healthy."

The fourth servants go away. Max also took his road.

If you are confident and stubborn, you will achieve your goals

When Max arrived in the village, he noticed a house located a considerable distance away, prompting him to seek refuge there. An old man lived there and agreed to give him shelter for the night. After he woke up, he saw that the old man had prepared breakfast for him. The man was sitting outside under a tree and looking at the village. Behind the village lay a mountain that was extremely difficult to climb.

Max had breakfast and set down next to the white-bearded old man to thank him for the shelter and the meal. Before that, he had left a few pennies on the bed as a reward for the hospitality. The old man looked at Max and invited him to stay with him until dinner, where he could watch the brave and strong young men from the village attempt to climb the mountain today. Every year on this day they are trying to climb the mountain because there is growing a wonderful bush, the color of which is healing. They made tea from flowers, which helps to treat many diseases. Suddenly, the bells rang, revealing that people were leaving their houses and making their way to the foot of the mountain. There, the entire village gathered to watch the strong men ascend the mountain. When they encountered more challenging situations, some of them resisted and returned. While some women persisted, others began yelling their husbands' names.

"Enough, you'll fall; get off."

Later on, the older people started shouting, and mothers begged their children to refuse because it was dangerous. Some men refused, but others continued. However, the screams of those at the bottom grew louder and more terrifying. Only a few men remained, determined to continue climbing. However, the crowd below was encouraging them to decline the climb, citing its impossibility and potential risks. One by one, the men faced rejection. Only a young man continued climbing. When people found out that only one young man left, they calmed down, stopped shouting, and went home. The old man and Max caught sight of him as he ascended to the top. The old man then approached Max and struck up a conversation with him.

"It's been going on for years. Since I moved to this village to live in. I am watching them every year. The first years, I admired that they were trying to achieve what they wanted. But after the second year, I climbed all the way to the top. On the other side, the climb is less strenuous, and almost anyone can reach the top. Subsequently, I explored a village located on the mountain's opposite side. I came to understand that they meticulously gather flowers from the bushes each year, prepare tea, and then sell it to other kingdoms. I asked them, "Is it possible that we from our village can come here to collect as much as we need from the flowers?"

They told me, "It's all right; just do not destroy the bush."

"The issue lies in the fact that the impact of these exquisite flowers is contingent upon their collection on this particular day. People from my village must travel to their village and work together to gather as many flowers as possible while ensuring that the bushes are not damaged. That we can do it also every next year. I asked the village, "Why not go around the mountain to the village on the other side after you returned?" From there, you can get to the top. The majority of the responses stated that there is no such village, and even if there were, it would take five days to reach another village. If they gather together, they should not share it because they should make tea and sell it abroad, and they gave many other excuses not to try. To the question of why we have struggled to climb the mountain from the more arduous part, they were saying, "We know that a long time ago, there was a man from our village who was able to do it; that is the easiest way." The young man who managed to climb the mountain is deaf-mute, and this is his second visit to the area. Last year, after successfully climbing the mountain, he returned a week later, carrying a couple of bottles containing tea with him. He is unable to explain how other villagers discovered him upstairs, brought him back to their village, and then guided him home. When this young man was a child, he observed what these people were doing every year and felt that his goal was to climb to the top, which became his dream. He harbored a deep-seated desire, like a seed planted in his mind, that one day, when he grew up, he would climb to the top and succeed. For many years, his only thought was that he would succeed; he had self-imposed courage and confidence. His imagination was working on how he would succeed, but what to do next, he doesn't know because he doesn't hear. After his first return, no villager explored how he got home or what he saw. "He is deaf-mute, so don't waste time on him," is the common response from people. He succeeded because he didn't hear the threatening calls or the pessimism they preached, which included threats and equanimity. Last year, after he returned home, I started teaching this young man how to read people's lips. I'm not sure how much he learned, but to some extent, he understood what I was saying. I attempted to explain the situation to him before he stood up to collect the bag. He rises to observe the actions of his fellow villagers. If they gather, he will follow their lead. When they depart, keep in mind the path they took and the method they used to prepare the tea. Let them make the tea there and then return to our village. When he gets home, I'll help him sell the bottle of elixir. More specifically, I will assist him in learning the art of selling. It would be beneficial for him to learn how to navigate life and avoid becoming a beggar in his village. And then I will tell him not to climb from this side, to climb it from another village, and from there go to collect the flowers, and everything he has to do he already knows. Should he exhibit stubbornness and comprehend the importance of adhering to a safe path, he will gain respect and value for his actions. I hope that he will come next week, and I will continue to teach him to face and body language."

Max wrote down the words of the white-bearded old man and memorized them in his memory.

"I see you can write; a few people on this world can write; only the people from the great kingdom can write."

"You're right, I come from the great kingdom, but is it really true that only a few people can write?"

"As far as I know, every kingdom has not so many people who can write."

"How is it possible? Don't they teach their children literacy and knowledge?"

"In most kingdoms, this is a crime, because kings don't need smart people because they think that they can threaten their thrones."

"So far, I have traveled extensively throughout the

kingdoms and witnessed a tremendous deal of misery. Every kingdom boasts a few wealthy individuals, while the majority live in extreme poverty. How are the kings planning to improve their lives?"

"That's the problem: they don't want to improve their lifestyle, but they want their people to be poor because they are easy to manage, and sometimes they give them a piece of bread as a celebration, and that's all."

"But the kings are the ones who lose; when the population is impoverished, they receive less and pay less taxes because they have nothing to give."

"That's true, but their happiness stems from always having the biggest basket at the dinner table. They don't have restless souls, which is why they keep their people impoverished. They pamper their merchants, ensuring they have enough for their daily needs. The merchants are solely concerned with their winnings, concealing their wealth behind the king's authority."

"But this is a vicious circle for humanity, and one day there will not be a future without poverty and disease."

"You are right, young man, but this is the reality."

Max stood up, and he slung the bag over his shoulder.

"Thank you for your hospitality and conversation. Stay healthy."

"I wish you good health and a good journey."

The Lord gives, but we must make an effort to take it

 As Max passed by the apple tree, he noticed a ten-year-old boy crying. He approached him and inquired, "Hi, boy, What's wrong? Why are you crying?"

"Hello, my father always tells me that if I really want something, I have to pray to the Lord ten times and it will come true. Every day, I pray to become as wealthy as the rich children, to own a huge horse, and to have a better home. Today, I prayed to the Lord to grant me the best apple from the top of the tree to eat, but something seems to be amiss; even the apple does not fall down. Lord doesn't seem to like me."

Max quietly pulled a coin out of his pocket and picked up a stone from the ground. He held a coin in one hand and a stone in the other hand.

"Tell me, which one you will choose?" Asked Max.

"The coin," said the boy.

"Ask Lord ten times that you want coin," said Max.

The boy repeated, "Lord, please, I want this coin!" ten times.

"See?" Max said. "Even if you say a thousand times a day that you chose a coin, it will not be yours. You have to reach out and take it. Simply speaking is insufficient; you must take action. Reach out and take the coin." The boy reached out and took the coin.

"See, it's yours now. Consider how to get the best apple from the top of the tree; if it's hard, ask for help; and find a stick. But first, you have to think about and then act on what you want. If you don't succeed today, I'm sure you will succeed tomorrow. You'll find a way to succeed. That's why I won't take it upon myself. You've got to find the way. It's not offensive to ask for help. Sometimes we need help, but don't forget to thank God for it. Sometimes we have to take risks to succeed. Without risks, we can't get what we want. It's one thing to want it, and it's another thing to achieve it. Preparation is crucial for achieving the goal. What does the term "preparedness" mean? When we express our desires to the Lord, we direct our attention and concentration toward this crucial matter for us. To do what we want, we need to prepare very well. How to do it? For instance, gathering knowledge on how to bring our desires to life is crucial. Achieving your goals becomes much faster if your motivation is strong and your intentions are clear and prepared. It doesn't matter if you want an apple or a lovely house. It's all about character. The habits you are building now will accompany you throughout your life. Your father correctly instructed you to pray ten times, anticipating that you would take action to fulfill your wish. The more information you narrow down, the more direction you are taking. The more effort you put in, whether physically or mentally, the sooner you achieve your desire. Sometimes, a person's belief that the goal is unattainable may not always hold true. Working hard and focusing results in the fog lifting, obstacles falling away, and reaching the goal. If you are ready, it will be easier for you to reach the goal. Good luck and all the best. God bless you."

Max took his own path while the child sat there, watching the coin in his hand.

The most difficult words to say are "thank you" and "sorry"

When Max arrived at the next location, he felt a sense of cleanliness and orderliness. He asked the first person he saw where he could stay for the night, to which he replied that everyone could shelter him, but it would be better to go to the richest house in the village.

As he walked, he marked a house that was larger than the others. He knocked and asked, "Hello, can I get a room and food? I will pay." Max asked.

"Welcome, of course, we will give you a shelter and food," the hostess replied. She guided him to a room located at the end of the corridor. It was a clean and tidy room. He left his bag, rested for ten minutes in bed, and went to the hostess for dinner. When he went next to them, he noticed that everything was clean and tidy, but there was one door that was full of nail holes; it was hanging on the wall like a big painting. He took a seat at the table, and the hostess arranged the dishes for him and the others, after which they started eating.

They enjoyed a quiet dinner, but Max frequently glanced at the door hanging on the wall.

After they had finished their meal, the housewife cleaned the table, filled two pitchers with sherbet, and placed them on the table—one in front of Max, the other one in front of her husband. She wished them a pleasant evening and went to her chambers.

"Tell me, young boy, what is your name? Where are you from? Where are you going?" The landlord asked.

"My name is Max; I travel around the kingdoms for a short time and write stories that I have seen happen or that I decide are interesting for me." Max answered.

"I noticed that you frequently glance at the door hanging on the wall; do you believe it has a story to tell?" The landlord asked.

Based on the room's unique furnishings and layout, I believe it holds significant value for you. To be there, I think it should remind you of something important that you've been through in your life." Max replied.

"I totally agree with you, Max; it serves as a reminder of my life's journey, and I'm delighted to share the story when someone visits my house. I was young. I had a sharp and unyielding temper. I often found myself involved in conflicts and scandals with others. I was often rude and offended them. One day my father gave me a bag full of nails and told me, "Son, I want to ask you something. Every time you fight with someone or insult them, stick a nail in the door in the yard."

"On the first day, I hammered twenty nails into the door. The second day I hammered twenty-two nails. In the days that followed, I started to reflect on each specific situation where I needed to hammer a nail. This led me to slow down, hammer fewer nails, and gradually learn to control my outbursts. That's how the pies stocked on the door slow down. The day arrived when I managed to avoid leaving even a single nail on the door. Then I went to my father and proudly told him about my achievement and what had happened to me."

He responded, "Very well, my boy. Now I want you to do something else. Every time you master your character, say a kind word to someone, or apologize for your previous rudeness, remove one of the stocked nails."

"I did just that. I started pulling the nails out of the door one by one, until the day came when there were none left. I immediately boasted to my father that I had succeeded. My father then led me to the door and complimented me, saying, "Son, you did a fantastic job with the tasks I gave you. You became a more reserved and positive person. Now, observe the numerous holes in the door; it will never return to its previous state. When you offend someone or behave rudely, you inflict pain on them, just as hammering a nail on a door causes pain to a tree. Even if you apologize and ask for forgiveness, the wound scars and door holes remain after you remove all the nails. Remember that with words, you can make a more serious wound on a person than a knife. Even if this wound heals, it will always leave a scar." I then realized that people will only remember me for the negative things I did, so I must ensure that they remember me only for the good things. I started helping out at my father's restaurant. For the diligence I put in, he paid me. I began saving money. When I learned that someone in the village needed assistance, I made sure to arrive first. I was the first to assist in digging their vineyard or clearing their harvest from the terraces. If the potter needed assistance bringing clay to the lonely man to sing wood, I was the first to volunteer. Interestingly, every time I assisted someone, I learned something new and valuable. Every soul has something in it: a seed of hope, faith, and love, regardless of whether one is poor, bad, or good. A few years later, others had already recognized me as a decent man. My perspective shifted, and I felt a sense of usefulness and satisfaction when I made someone else happy. I greeted everyone that I met. I paused beside each craftsman, observing their work from a distance, identifying areas for improvement or simplification, and encouraging them to give it a try. In numerous instances, I have extended financial assistance to those in need, yet I remain uncertain whether divine intervention or chance has contributed to my wealth and improved quality of life. I have helped many craftsmen to increase their production of the goods and to sell more to other villages. At some point, I started helping people from neighboring villages. A few villages have merged, and we now have a merchant representative in the free zone of the great kingdom. We maintain a few stalls, earn enough money to save, and donate a portion of it to the less fortunate individuals in these villages. From what I have experienced so far, I have learned that a person makes the choice of what it should be and can always change it by choosing a new goal. It's not easy to choose something new, but my goal was to remember myself only by doing good things. That is a great goal, but it takes a lot of persistence. I earned the respect and love of others, but I had to first earn it myself. If you want to get it, first you have to give it to yourself. The most difficult words to say from the heart are "thank you" and "sorry," but when they become a habit, your life becomes more calm and harmonious. Thank you for being my guest. Get a good night's sleep, and I'll see you tomorrow at breakfast, and you'll get food for the road." Max also thanked him for his hospitality, and he went to sleep.

It's hard to win a real friend, but it's easy to lose a friend

 Max arrived in the next kingdom and stayed in the closest village near the castle—in the house where a wise man had been living. In the evening, the host gave him a meal and showed him the bedding where he could sleep. When Max woke up in the morning and saw that he had breakfast, he washed and then sat down to eat. The old man was sitting in front of his house, watching the sun set over the horizon. Max had just finished his breakfast and sat down next to the old man to thank him before continuing his travel. During this time, a young man approached the old man for advice and posed the following intriguing question, "I'd like to know how many friends a person should have.

I thought a lot about the proverb: "It's better to have a hundred friends than a hundred gold coins." While the proverb holds some truth, I believe that pursuing a large number of friends can lead to insincerity and false emotions. Time tests friendships, as it can be challenging to truly understand a new acquaintance and find the strength and time to cultivate a hundred friends.

"I can provide you with the answer," the sage said. "I would prefer to assist you in comprehending the answer independently. Have you noticed the large apple tree in the yard? I want to ask you to bring me an apple from the top."

The man looked up, shielded his eyes from the harsh sun, and inquired. "But how do I do it? The apple is actually very high."

"Ask your friend to help you. Perhaps together you can reach the highest branch of the tree," said the old man.

So the man did it. He went and took his friends; they started climbing on each other's shoulders, but it didn't help to climb the tree.

"It cannot happen," he sadly said.

"Don't you have more friends?" asked the wise man with a smile.

Other men, who were his friends, attempted to climb over each other to reach the top of the tree, but each fell, got up, and tried again, only to fail. After multiple unsuccessful attempts, all of his friends eventually left him; only one remained, silently standing on the ground.

The wise man summoned the young man and spoke to him.

"Now do you understand how many friends a person should have in their life?"

"Yes, teacher, thank you. I understood it all. We should cultivate as many friends as possible to tackle every problem together."

The wise man sadly shook his head, turned around, and said, "I guess it's nice to have a lot of friends. But perhaps it's more important to have one or two smart friends who know how to solve a problem. For example, he might consider bringing a ladder to reach the top of the tree. This is the difference between a true friend and a not-true friend. You must have at least one best friend, two or three trustworthy friends, and as many other friends as you want. A trustworthy friend from whom you can learn new things in life to move forward might also be older than you; even he/she can be a parent, relative, or craftsman. A trustworthy friend will listen to you without interrupting or regretting your emotions and feelings. A trustworthy friend encourages you to be content and to pursue your goals. No matter the situation, a trustworthy friend will never abandon you during a challenging period. He will support you because he believes in you and wants you to succeed. A true friend will only look for you when they miss you. The not-real friend will only look for you when he needs your help. A real friend knows how important it is to be alone from time to time. An insincere friend will try to attract most of your time. A true friend will be delighted to invite you to celebrate your success. The real friend is sympathetic. A true friend knows that everyone has different types of friends and won't judge you for it. An insincere friend will not like your friends. A true friend accepts you for who you are. A non-sincere friend tries to control you and change you. A true friend respects both himself and yourself. A best friend is someone who treats you with everything I've told you so far. However, this relationship must be reciprocal. You can always rely on him, and vice versa. Now it's up to you to choose your friends."

The young man looked surprised and silent.

"Now I get it—how many and what kind of friends I need. Thank you for the lesson that you gave to me; I'll remember it." Max was able to record everything that happened. "Thank you, wise man, for your hospitality and may your health continue to improve." Max went his own way.

What we say or do is the result of our thoughts

 Max was walking along the path to the top of the mountain. He had almost reached the top and was just walking to find his next step when a woman with two children appeared.

"Hi, I went up to the top to see if there was a village near here where I could stay for the night."

"Hello, young man! There is; I'll show you, but first we must climb the mountain to teach my kids." The woman replied. "Children need to learn one of life's most important lessons, as they often fight and offend each other. Despite their father's efforts to impart all his knowledge, his daily routine of cutting wood in the forest and selling it to earn money for our daily needs has taken up his time. But now, I think it's time for a big lesson about life's rules—what to do and how."

They were already at the top. There was a beautiful view from the top. Max and the children stood there and were watching the beauty. It looks like the time has stopped. The boys kept talking about how everything was so wonderful, how small their village looked, how close the sky is... The mother waited until the boys stopped talking, then smiled and said, "Yes, children, now I want you to do something. Take a deep breath and shout with all your strength: I hateee you!"

The children looked surprised and then turned their gaze to their mother, who invited them to do it with her eyes.

"I hateee you!" they shouted with all their straight at the same time.

"I hateee you! I hateee you! I hateee you!" answered the echo.

"And now I want to shout: I lovee you!" the mother said.

The kids did it, and the echo answered them, "I loveee you! I loveee you! I loveee you!"

The mother went near her children and hugged them.

"Now, children, you have learned one of the rules of life: you get only what you give. If you view the world with anger and hate, you will receive the same. If you look at the world with love, you will get love and support. Remember that lesson, children: live as you want, but better with love. Each of us is fighting with himself/herself. An angel and a devil are fighting in our souls.

The evil devil embodies anger, envy, incompleteness, denial, greed, arrogance, self-regret, feelings of inferiority or superiority, lies, false pride, selfishness, laziness, and all other qualities that are detrimental to

45

humanity. The good angel embodies joy, peace, love, hope, calmness, modesty, kindness, benevolence, reciprocity, generosity, sincerity, compassion, faith, and all the qualities that are beneficial to others.

The children thought for a moment and then asked their mother, "Who wins the angel or the devil?"

"The one you consistently feed up will ultimately prevail. If you continue to use bad words and think like a devil, your actions will become like those of the devil, and people will see you in this sight. But if you use only beautiful words, from the bottom of your heart, of course, and your thoughts coincide with the qualities of an angel, I hope that your actions will also be in your favor. You will always be handsome and smiling; people will respect and appreciate you; and you will be an angel. Now let's go back."

They went to the village. When they arrived, the woman invited Max to spend the night with them, after which he could continue his journey tomorrow. Max accepted the invitation with pleasure. Before Max went to bed, the children's father returned, and they engaged in a conversation. Before he went to sleep, he wrote down today's story. In the morning, he left satisfied, leaving three coins under the bedsheets of the hostess.

To forgive means to clear yourself of the burden of your soul

Max was near a castle in the next kingdom, which had a house located very close to its wall. The house was clean and tidy, and he went there. When he arrived, he saw an old woman cleaning outside.

"Hello, young boy!" the old woman welcomes him.

"Hello!" he answered.

"From where are you coming and where are you going?" asked the old lady.

"I am traveling around the kingdoms, and today I came here. I have to find a shelter for tonight and food for the next couple of days."

"We can provide you with shelter, and you can purchase food from the nearby stands. Come sit and have a rest. Soon my husband will come back."

"What is your husband working? Your house is very close to the castle; I don't believe that everyone can."

"You are right, my son. My husband is a very fair and wise man. Many people seek his advice to resolve their problems. When he became famous, the King ordered us to relocate here. He wants us to live close to him so that he can ask my husband for advice when he needs it, rather than relying on his advisors. He will be back soon." Max was finishing his writing when the wise man returned.

"You are welcome, young boy! It is time for dinner. Come join with us. Let see what my lovely wife had prepared."

"Thank you! Your wonderful wife has also offered me a place to stay tonight. I hope that you will be alright with that."

"No, it is fine. Come to sit with us."

Max sat with them, and they had dinner. While they were enjoying their dinner, Max noticed a man hurriedly approaching the house. He arrived and asked the old man, "Tobias, wise man, please help me; I cannot suffer any more like that."

"You are welcome. Come to eat, and then we will speak."

He refused and said, "I cannot eat and drink because I cannot find peace in my soul."

The old man had already finished with the dinner and washed his hands and his mouth with a towel. He turned to the young man and asked him to share his pain, but to speak slowly.

Before a month passed, a fight broke out between my child and the child of my best friend while they were playing on the road. Accidentally, while I was getting over, I saw that my child was crying while the other kid was laughing. Suddenly I felt very angry. Without asking what was going on or giving it any thought, I entered my friend's home without his permission and slapped him. I left peacefully without saying anything to him. At the beginning of our relationship, I felt content with myself, but then my anguish overcame me. No matter what I do, my consciousness remains. All month I cannot calm myself. Despite my best efforts, I was unable to achieve the desired results. I observed that the kids, who had been in a conflict, had now resumed their play. Even without a friend to confide in, I find myself struggling to communicate my issues. Please help me.

The wise man was silent for around a minute and said, "Can you see that stone under the tree? I want you to hold and carry it as much as possible. Proceed to the well, then to the tree, then to the river, and continue this process until you reach a point where you are unable to carry it any longer. When that moment comes, come back to me."

In his despair, the man immediately picked up the stone, which appeared large and awkward to carry, and proceeded to the well. While the man was carrying the stone to the well, an old man approached him. Suppose the man gets exhausted from carrying that stone and comes back.

While Max was watching how the man was carrying it to the tree and to the river and had already started to slow it down, he said, "Maximum one hour."

Tobias, the old man, watched at him and said, "Even earlier."

While they were speaking, the man came back after half an hour through the stone on the ground and said very tiredly, "If I continue carrying it, my hands will break or my legs will weaken. Even more tiredness could cause me to lose consciousness and potentially die.

"You free yourself alone from the stone. I did not tell you to do it. Similarly, you can break free from your struggles. You can ask your friend to forgive you for the slap. You know why you slapped him. Did he know why you did it? Moreover, he might be struggling more while he is searching for a reason why you slapped him. His spiritual burden may be bigger than yours. The only way is to go to him and ask for forgiveness. Furthermore, expressing your remorse to him will lessen your burden, and reciprocating his forgiveness will also lessen his. Both of you will remove the burden from your soul, just as you did with the stone. When you forgive each other, you leave the pain in the past, putting an end to your internal conflicts. You will be free of internal battles with yourself, and you will not harbor anger, hatred, or guilt. If you forgive with your heart, soon you will forget about all that. If you are strong, you will ask for forgiveness. Forgiveness is a road of friendship and amity for you. I can help you only with my advice. You need to complete the remaining tasks."

"Thank you, Tobias, wise man. Now I will go visit my friend."

He did not wait for goodbye and ran to the village.

The old man, Tobias, turned to Max and said, "We humans are not without faults. Sometimes the anger and hate within us take over, and when that happens, we have a tendency to hurt others. That is in our nature. In such moments, we often neglect to reflect, empathize with others, or deliberate our actions based solely on our own egos and anger, which ultimately leads to our own misery. Now, let's go to sleep because tomorrow I will go to a village to solve one conflict, which I accepted to help. Good night." Max also wished him a peaceful night, wrote the story to which he was a witness, and went to sleep.

Joy is an inspiration for optimism and energy

In the morning, when they woke up, the old Tobias had to go to the next village.

"Can we go there together, and then I'll continue?" Max asks.

"Of course you can," said Tobias.

As they strolled along the road, the wise man and Max observed and discussed the stunning surroundings. They passed by a yard and observed a farmer at work. The man was working hard, sweat running down his forehead, and he was moaning from the fatigue. There was a tree next to it. The wise Tobias went to the tree, invited Max to follow him, and started speaking to the farmer.

"Hey, man, let's sit in the shade and talk and rest a little."

"I can't. I need to work. I have so much work to do."

"Why do you work so hard?" asked the wise Tobias.

"Stop resting from time to time. Look what a wonderful day it is!"

"I can't. I don't have time to enjoy my day or my life," replied the man sadly.

"But why do you doom yourself to all that?" asked the old man, Tobias.

"So, you're missing out on the fun of the view, the weather, and the natural need to rest."

"I don't have time for these things! Work and suffering are necessary to make my children and grandchildren happy. My grandfather did the same for my father, and my father suffered because of me.

"Was anyone in your family happy?" asked the wise man.

"Not yet, but my children and grandchildren will surely be!" the man exclaimed, and he continued his work.

"Look, buddy... Let me give you some advice. How can a blind man teach us to see? How can a deaf person teach us to hear? How can a mute teach us to speak? How will the person who does not have knowledge teach us? You say that your relatives also worked and suffered. The same thing happens to you now. First, learn the joys of life. Laughing and savoring the sun's rays as it rises, shines, or sets, the wind, the rain that instills hope, and the breathtakingly beautiful land that provides us with everything are all part of the experience. The Lord created everything around us. You are sad at heart. If you are sad at heart, then your mind is dark. If your mind is dark, your body is not so healthy. And your family is unhappy, too. First of all, learn to use our gifts, which we can get without money. Having more fun will give you the strength to overcome everything much more easily. Then they will also give you more ideas, such as what to sow this year or divide into two levels and plant two crops. Firstly, you must cultivate happiness so that you can impart this to your children. Only with joy there is happiness. If you smile every day for five minutes, you will experience joy and happiness. I wish you from the bottom of my heart to be healthy and happy."

The farmer had stopped and didn't know what to do. Max and the wise man left and got back on the road.

"Most people avoid the joys that can inspire them to live a better life. They miss what's right in front of them," added the wise man.

When you are helping other people, you are also helping to yourself

 They arrived in the village where they were waiting for the wise Tobias. Max also joined the crowd. The wise man went in front of the people and invited them to tell him their problem.

A man began to speak to Tobias: "We always have difficulties that stop us from achieving our goals and distract us from our daily activities. We begin a task, only to find ourselves unable to complete it due to unforeseen circumstances that divert our attention. We start working, but something happens, and we cannot finish what we had started. We constantly mumble, "This is not good," and we always assign blame to someone else for what we did not accomplish. In short, we only complain that it doesn't work; we don't trust ourselves. Where is our problem?"

"All right, bring me a very big rock that at least four people can move," said Tobias.

The men who were in front immediately started talking about where the nearest rock was and went there to take it. A hundred meters from the downtown area, a sizable chunk of rock was visible.

55

A dozen men pushed him and rolled him to the center, right in front of everyone's eyes. Tobias instructed them to leave it directly in front of the store.

"Now, what do you see?" Tobias spoke while a large rock blocked the store's entrance and exit.

"One big rock," some people replied.

"That's one of your difficulties. Why? Your visit to the store will be hindered. The store employee is also unable to enter. He can't deliver the goods or pick them up. Now, will you leave him to cope alone with that problem? You are witnesses to the fact that one person cannot solve the problem alone. How are you going to do?"

"Well, we have to help him," the man said.

"That's right, you have to help him—not just him, but everyone who is carrying goods for sale and everyone who goes to the store for shopping. In other words, deciding the problem benefits everyone. Recognizing that a single individual cannot accomplish the task, whether it's a neighbor, friend, or acquaintance, it's crucial for you to assist one another. If you assist one person, they will reciprocate, making it easier for all of you to help each other. You are not only helping others, but you are also helping yourself. If a neighbor is successful, your family benefits. If you have a lot of apples in the yard, pass the basket to your neighbor. If he had many eggs, he would share. Helping yourself means that the difficulties become invisible, and life becomes more pleasant. However, if you interfere with each other, your life becomes difficult and unbearable. Your village makes pottery. Everyone begins their work in their respective workshops without a common goal. Once you are tired, you go to your neighbor, who is also working. Your conversation with him disrupts and hinders his work. Because you didn't finish your work when you returned, you had to start over from scratch. Instead of using your time to complete your task on time, you wasted it. Your neighbor is in the same position. Every subsequent product fails to meet your expectations, and you realize they're unable to provide you with a competitive price. Emotionally, you are upset and unhappy. It affects your family relationships. The next day, your wife made a breakfast you didn't like, and the circus closed. Every day we make decisions that are either significant or not so significant. Each choice you make will have an impact on your future. Eliminate the justification of blaming someone or something else for your laziness. You made a mistake, which you are now trying to rectify. Recharge yourself with optimism, a medicine you will need for the day after tomorrow. With a powerful force, believe in yourself, take the fight, and I'm sure you will succeed. At night, once you've completed your work, you can relax and prepare yourself for the next day. This way, everyone will succeed."

"Thank you for coming; we'll do our best. We can see what will happen." The crowd went home.

"I hope you understand, Max, that everyone carries a stone in their soul or in their hand. I realized that there was an obstacle in his path, like the rock. But a person has a choice: leave it or wear it. You can either knead a stone from the road alone, or you can do it with assistance. However, to move forward unencumbered by burdens and obstacles, you must remove them without hindering others. I wish you all the best." said Tobias and went to the road that leads to his house.

If you want to stop drinking, look at the nondrinker

 Max is staying at a hotel. At one of the tables, people were conversing with each other. Many of the men were intoxicated. Meanwhile, two of the king's people came in. And announced the desire of the king.

"We will reward anyone who finds a cure for the king's headache."

A man under the influence of alcohol asked, "What gives him the headache? He has everything, and he doesn't care about anything."

Then one of the king's men answered, "The king likes to have fun. Almost every evening, he gathers his noble friends and engages in activities such as eating, drinking, and having fun until late at night. He eventually grew accustomed to consuming copious amounts of wine. Wine makes him talkative, playful, and extremely fun. This became pleasant for him, and he began to get drunk often. However, once he becomes intoxicated, the king experiences severe discomfort in the morning hours. His mouth burns, and his head aches to the point of breaking. He doesn't want anyone to talk to him, as everything irritates and exacerbates his anger. Therefore, he decreed that whoever brought him a medicine to help him feel better after drinking would receive a great reward."

The man immediately said, "If so, we will help him."

"How?" asked one of the King's men.

"Take me there to be sure that I will get my reward. And let a few men come with me, to be sure that you won't lie to me."

The king's men accompanied them to the palace. Max also joined the other men to see what happens. They entered the palace and told the king they had brought someone to identify his morning medicine. The King approached the hall, where several people were present, and inquired.

The king said, "Where is the medicine? Tell me. What steps can I take to avoid getting sick after drinking?

"Continue with the same alcohol that you were drinking at night," the half-dunked man replied.

"What do you mean?" the king wondered.

"My devout king, have you ever heard the saying: One wedge knocks out another? Drink and don't be afraid. If it doesn't work, remove my head."

"Well, if I continue like this all the time, how far can I go?" asked the King.

"So far as I get," answered the half-dunked man.

The king was speechless. His eyes widened, and he looked at the man with horror. His face was dark and swollen, his nose was black and blue, his eyes were bulging like frogs, his clothes were dirty and splattering—all of this was so ugly and disgusting that he screamed, "Give him a reward and let him get out of my sight. He really healed me."

"At least I've already cut it. I promise not to put any alcohol in my mouth." And he returned to his chambers.

The group of people waited for their friend to pick up the purse with gold money and returned to the hotel. And there the fun began. Max was with them, too. He ate and went to bed. He finished his notes and went to bed. In the morning, the ongoing fun kept him awake. He went down to the boys to see if they were still upright. He observed that some boys were sleeping on tables, others were on the ground, and some were still drinking and singing. Some of them woke up and started drinking again. He saw a woman who was carrying her husband to their house. He had already paid his bills and went to help the woman. She happily agreed, because her husband was kicking his feet and was almost inadequate.

Max said, "It looks like your husband won't be able to go to work today."

"Oh, my boy, it's not just today; until they run out of money, perhaps all the men won't be working for a month."

"Why?" Max asked.

"There is a true that people are saying: Where there is a stupid king, the people are also stupid. When our king started drinking, and his men also became alcoholizers. But the news quickly spreads. Let us hope that our King will refrain from his sins, allowing men to prioritize their families, as women and children are facing extreme poverty. The sober pays for the sins of the drunken." They arrived at the woman's house. "Thank you very much, young man, and let God protect you," the woman said.

And Max went to another kingdom.

It is difficult to remain silent, it is important to listen and understand

 A huge shout echoed next to a small river at the edge of the village. Max stepped forward and went to see and hear what was happening to the group of people. As soon as he arrived, he saw two groups of people, each armed with wooden sticks and ready to fight at any moment. They were shouting at each other so loudly that they didn't understand anything.

In less than a few minutes, a group of people, led by an elderly man, arrived from the village. They entered between the two groups, left the old man in the middle, and went to the back. Then everyone became quiet. It looks like the old man had the authority and respect to shut everyone up. The old man sat down on the ground and invited everyone to sit down with his hands. The two groups of people, along with those who had brought the old man, took their seats, and Max joined them. The old man took a deep breath, exhaled, and began to speak. "One of the most difficult things is to be silent. Asking questions is crucial for learning. I have the ability to listen and understand.

You can acquire valuable lessons from others by attentively listening and embracing the truth. It helps prevent misunderstandings during communication. Put yourself in other shoes; he is bothered with something, or he wants to say something that will be in your interests in the future. You need to learn how to listen. Can you understand someone if you don't finish the conversation? If someone respects, loves, and evaluates you, how will you know if they are bullying, humiliating you, underestimating you, or acting malevolently toward you? Listen to him until the end, draw conclusions, and then speak, but be careful not to fall into his trap. How do you know that he doesn't need your help or support? If you don't listen to him, how can you know he's not trying to help or protect you? People express their thoughts and feelings based on their own emotions. However, we must be tolerant enough to listen, understand, and conduct normal conversations. If you are able to listen and understand what they are saying, only then can a pleasant conversation lead to problem-solving. Never forget that everyone wants to say something; no matter what, just get around, listen, and you have a chance to learn something new or smart. When the prophets spoke, their followers listened intently and recorded their words, which is how we have gained more knowledge today.

Talking without listening prevents you from hearing anything that could solve the problem. This situation only escalates the conflict, potentially severing the relationships and causing harm. Many people like to talk to us, especially the wise old ones who can give advice. If you consider me a wise man, I simply enjoy listening to those who approach me. Over the years, I have developed the ability to listen attentively and communicate calmly and slowly. The difference between an ordinary person and a wise person is that only the first one knows how to listen, understand, and decide what advice to give so that our neighborhood will calm down and find a way to get what he or she wants without harming anyone or anything. We must draw that conclusion from our extensive life experience. Even I can learn a lot from a child. No one knows everything. Every person on earth is normal and has their own physiological needs. The only difference is that some people prefer to listen and learn through their experiences. If you understand that everything is incredibly simple, you can achieve success. However, no one is born knowing everything, and therefore, we must continuously learn throughout our lives. To gain knowledge, you must actively listen and comprehend. What you are doing now is no longer an argument but rather a step toward causing harm beyond just physical and mental injuries. My advice is to return home immediately, consider the potential consequences, and meet early tomorrow morning to discuss and resolve your issue." The old man stood up. The people who were with him assisted him, after which he proceeded towards the village. The two groups that were engaged in an argument halted their argument, stood up, and departed. Max suggested that, based on their conversation, the issue was a family issue, potentially even a breed issue. He got up and went his own way.

The envy is a waste of time and future

Max was walking towards the village. He noticed that the houses were not visible from the high fences. Finally, he spotted a wonderful unfenced house at the village's highest point. Young trees and flowers were planted in the yard. There was a breathtakingly beautiful gazebo nearby. He went there to inquire about a place to stay and where he could purchase food for his journey. Two little girls were playing in the yard. When they saw Max, both of them called their mom, "Mom, mom! Brother at the door."

A woman came, "Welcome, son. How can I help you?"

"Hello. I am traveling from kingdom to kingdom, from village to village, describing stories and anecdotes from people's lives. Now, I am in your village, where I can stay for the night and buy food for the road."

"Here, son. We will provide you with shelter and food. My husband will be back soon," she said, guiding Max to the room where he could spend the night.

"Enter the gazebo; I'll prepare a hot tea to help you combat the heat. The dinner will be ready in an hour."

He sat in the gazebo, took a sip of his tea, and transcribed his notes from the previous days. The owner appeared. They said "Hello". The host sat down and chatted about normal pleasantries. The owner's name was Sancho. When he learned that Max visits villages and writes stories, he offered Max the opportunity to share a poignant story about the village, one that would be beneficial to his family. They set the table for dinner, and both the hosts and the children sat down to begin eating. After they had finished, the hostess took the dinner, and the children went to play in the garden. Sancho began to tell his story.

"As you've noticed, every house in our village has a high fence. The peasants' yards and houses are hidden from view. How did we get here? In the village, people always talk about each other. Everyone found defects in others. They started having problems with each other. We had the reputation of being the most envious village. First everyone was saying bad things about other kingdoms, then about other villages, until they started saying bad things about their neighbors and finally their friends. From the simple envy, it became malice. There was no normal life in the village. At the nights they started jumping inside other houses and were poisoning the neighbor's pets because their pets looked more fended.

Or he had more goats or chickens in their baskets. The neighbor's apple had more fruits. Seedlings have more roots of tomatoes or cucumbers. Nothing could make them less envious. All this information became known within the palace. Not a single tree remains in the family gardens. The king sought advice from wise men from other villages, and they arrived at a conclusion. He decided to visit the village. He arrived in the village with his advisors. He was sitting in a large tent here and ordered each family to go talk to him separately. Each man and his wife will stand for a maximum of ten minutes and must answer the king's question. They started from the oldest and youngest families. Finally, after we had all passed, the king stood in the center of the village and began to speak, saying, I've told you all that I am willing to give or do something in exchange for telling me at least one other family that can make or give twice as much as your family. My advisors recorded everyone's wishes in writing. In order to fulfill your wishes, half of the village must be without hands, property, eyes, legs, etc. I thought of offering you something that anyone would want—at least a purse full of gold or a new home, but you had to name at least one family to give them twice as much as to your family. But your answers are impossible. Rather than what I anticipated, I received responses akin to "cutting off one eye for myself and two for the other family" or "pulling out one eye for me and both hands for the other family." Envious people are willing to suffer if they know that others will suffer even more.

I am confident that if I offer you a monthly fee of one hundred pennies for working with me and I offer your neighbor ninety pennies, you will agree. However, if I were to offer you a monthly fee of one hundred and twenty pennies and your neighbor a monthly fee of one hundred and thirty, you would not accept it. You didn't even present it as an option to the other family. Sancho's family is the poorest, I suppose, but he is not like you. But in fact, Sancho wishes a good house with a beautiful garden, and to whom to make two wonderful houses, the answer was, "I prefer you to do it for every family or to do it for nobody; I do not want to offend anyone from my neighbors." So I decided the following: His new house, with its beautiful garden, will be the only one visible every day, free from any fence. I order you to raise your fences above the human eye. You can't see what your neighbor has and is doing. As compensation for all houses, you will receive money, which you can use to purchase materials for your fences. Additionally, as a bonus, I will construct a fence at the village's end and give you a hundred cows as payment. Your village has two hundred people. Your nightly task will be to milk a different cow while Sancho shepherds them. You will know that each family owns a half cow, but not all of it. Your neighbor or friend, with whom you spend the evening, will share half of the milk, forcing you to understand that food is essential for survival. Your malicious envy is invisible grief, destructive, and the reason you are unhappy and harm only yourself.

You understand that I am the King, so why are you jealous of me? Envy is an emotion that conveys inner anger stemming from the success, joy, satisfaction, and well-being of others. I didn't even know that you existed until yesterday. We hope that you will prosper and become one of the world's wealthiest villages if you succeed in establishing a prosperous community. If that doesn't happen, I'm unsure of how to proceed. Be healthy, and I hope you will succeed. The King did what he said; he built me a house with a garden and gave people money to build their fences. We've been doing this for two years. Every night the women come to milk the cows. Then men started coming in to get laid with the cows. And now this year we have 70 calves. It's likely that people have come to understand what is common, not just for themselves, but for everyone. Not yet, but when the King sees that people respect each other, he may let them remove the fences. I hope that this day will come soon.

The geed has no measures

 Max arrived before evening in the king's kingdom of Chen. There were people who had gathered at the palace gates. Everyone was waiting. The elderly, women, and children made up the majority of the crowd.

Max proceeded and entered the walls of the palace. There was a huge table, and the king and his advisers were sitting there. Several other individuals were also seated on the gown.

He saw an old man sitting far away from the crowd. He came and sat down next to him.

"Hi! What are all those people waiting for?" Max asked politely.

"Hello, young man, it seems you're clearly not from this kingdom and don't know what's going on," the old man responded. "For many years, that event of the year has been a tradition for the kingdom. Every year, everyone eagerly anticipates participating in these competitions at the same time. The villagers believe that the King bestows awards, but in reality, he holds all the greedy individuals accountable. The requirements are to enter as a participant, leave the palace gate in the morning, travel to the nearest forest with hazelnut trees, collect only leaves, and return to the palace gate before midnight. The King will reward you with coins equivalent to the kilograms of leaves you bring."

"Applause, you have a very generous king," Max exclaimed.

"From that perspective, it is indeed true. As greed has shown, there is always less or no money."

"Why do people look at it so greedily?" asks Max.

"My boy, a few years ago, before this event began, this king's grandfather personally attempted to estimate how much time you would need to travel to that hazelnut forest. How long it will take to return, and how much time for the collection. Additionally, upon your return, you will be carrying a heavy load, which may cause you to slow down due to fatigue."

"Well, I guess that if it's happening every year, people should have learned a lesson and know how to succeed," Max stated.

"You are thinking rationally, my boy, but that is the case with people who can believe in and find satisfaction in small things. Since then, from what I recall, about a dozen out of a thousand participants have achieved success. There have been participants who have only a few coins, others who have a wallet full of gold coins, and one participant who even managed to obtain two wallets of gold coins. However, in recent times, people often view success as a sign of courage."

"Everyone should succeed if others have succeeded before, and they should learn from them."

"Of course, it's one thing to learn and get the reward, but it's another to get greedier and not take anything. The greed is insatiable. The greed has no measure. It dominates you to the extent that you lose self-control. Thirst keeps you from being thirsty even more. Getting greedy destroys others and yourself. Unbridled greed destroys many people in this world. It was already midnight, and a man was just making his way into the palace yard. He managed to fit in the time, and people applauded him. They placed the bags containing the collected leaves on the scale, then positioned coins on the opposite side. On the seventeenth coin, the scales align perfectly. The money was enough for a year for the winner's family. Once the winner received the coins, everyone headed back to their homes. Some went to meet their men and bring them back, so they don't continue if they lost a measure of time."

The old man continued his conversation with Max, saying, "This man has been successful for several years, and I am sure that in a few months the king will invite him to work in the palace without other people knowing about that. The King, being wise, understands that this peasant is not greedy and knows how to handle such situations. He needs someone who is driven by the desire to succeed, and he is confident that greed will not fail him. He had demonstrated his abilities over a period of three years. Others, driven by their greed, strove to collect more leaves in order to earn more coins. Now they have no gold coins. If they had self-control and could control their greed, they could earn a few gold coins, which would be a plus for them and their families. This is the origin of the world, where greed thrives. Those who are grateful for the little they receive succeed, and eventually, life rewards them. More greed means more dissatisfaction and a miserable life.

You don't appear to be a local; I assume you don't have a place to stay. Please join me at my house, where I will provide you with food and a bed."

"With pleasure," Max said, getting up and following him.

What you sow is what you reap

 Max came to the village. However, he found a multitude of people weeping and sobbing in the village. Everywhere he looked, he could see quarrels and sad words emanating from the houses.

As he walked towards the end of the village, he came across a small house where an elderly man sat thoughtfully. Max went to him and asked.

"Hi, did something tragic happen in the village?"

"Hello, young man! Sit down. I will bring you a glass of water and answer your question. Two days ago, in the village, a woman went from house to house to tell us that she had a dream about death coming to our village and would take her soul with her. She spoke so convincingly that people believed her and became fearful. Fear compelled everyone to take actions that were not natural to them. In fact, two old men have died, three men and two children have their legs broken, and several women are in a big tragedy. Several patients lie on the bed, suffering from anxiety and fear. A person with a small mind sometimes sowed, without any thinking, more fear and anxiety. And those fears and anxieties grow bitter fruits.

76

When faced with unsatisfactory news, he tends to hold himself and his loved ones accountable. Bad rumors sometimes go the wrong way. Her house was the worst hit. Her father-in-law is dead, her husband has a broken arm, and her child has a broken leg. Fear, worry, and chaos are more prevalent than bad news—everyone is searching for a way to hide from death. Everyone knows that one day we will die, and we must accept death without fear. People want to live longer, even if they're unhappy. However, we must prioritize our health during our lifetime. Everyone wants health, but they do everything possible to deprive themselves of it. People don't take care of their bodies, don't play sports, eat well, laugh from the heart, or have fun. They allow fear to control their lives. They have to take care of themselves in order to spread happiness. They say they want happiness, but they refuse to see it when it is in their hands. Don't look at it while they're searching for something else— something bigger, something alien. They forget to enjoy the simple things in life. They forget that it is inside them that is the real happiness. They forget to smile. They forget to thank you. They forget to live. To show love. They say they want love, but they don't let it into their hearts. They create barriers, build walls, and install padlocks. They isolate themselves due to their fear of potential harm. In fact, it's self-harming. They try not to be robbed. Indeed, this is precisely how they deceive themselves. They may fear taking risks, but their true fear lies in life itself. To sow friendship.

They say they want real friendship but don't realize they must give it first. They don't understand that friendship is more than everyday communication. Friendship is support. Friendship is a power. Friendship is a division. Friendship is a willingness to swallow your pride when necessary. Friendship is readiness to help when needed. Friendship requires us to make selfless sacrifices when necessary. To spread hope for success. They express a need for success, but they are not prepared to put in the necessary effort. They are choosing fear before courage because they're afraid of failing. They choose security over the risk of change because they don't know what's coming next. They prefer to follow fate rather than draw it. They choose the role of observer instead of discoverer. They must acknowledge that the final decision lies with them.

I see you're a traveler; you can stay here for tonight. We'll find something to eat." The old man said it and went back to his home.

"Thank you!" Max said, and he followed him.

You can only give what you have

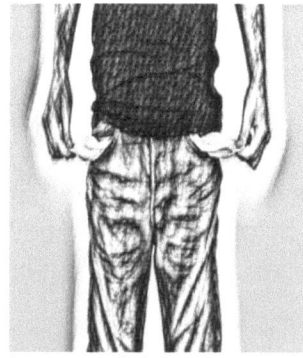 The following day, Max spotted a man sitting on a small lake, fishing.

He approached him, greeted him, and then settled down to rest. They engaged in a conversation, while a man on a ride approached them. The rider's clothing showed that he was rich.

It appears that the nobleman recognized the old man from the village and decided to stop.

"Dear Hans, if you are so intelligent, why aren't you wealthy?" asked the nobleman.

Hans turned to his rich, gold-trimmed cloak and responded.

"Listen to me, dear cloak; many people, especially the rich, think that I'm poor. But they are all wrong. I'm rich, but you can't see my wealth. It has no external manifestation; it is inside me." The nobleman held this man in high regard for his wisdom and intelligence, but it was evident that he was a madman. He remained silent and did not respond. And Hans continues talking to his clothes, "Now I will provide a more detailed explanation, dear Cloak. When your master goes to bed at night, he doesn't take you with him. Neither you, nor his servants, nor his gold are with him while he is sleeping. And if he dreams of a tiger chasing him, he will not call for help from his servants but will run. Only swift running will save him. If he dreams that he is alone in the middle of a snow field and is dying of cold, he will not be able to get rid of his expensive metal detector. The only thing that will save him is his ability to light a fire. Our abilities are our true wealth. They are inside us, and only their manifestations are outside."

The nobleman, already indignant that the wise man did not even address him but spoke to his clothes, shouted, "You are clearly not a wise man, but just a madman! How can you talk to my cloak? Can't you see me? I am speaking."

Hans smiled and said, "That's the way most people think. They talk to the bodies and do not see who their owners are. They see faces but rarely look into souls. They draw conclusions easily. It is possible that I am the largest merchant, dressed as a peasant, and fishing in order to avoid recognition or to be a tramp in my kingdom to observe the way in which my people live. People tend to focus solely on our clothing and packaging. If we were only naked, people might define us as higher, lower, weaker, or fatter, but our true selves are actually within us. We cannot perceive those things immediately. These things reside in our thoughts, in our souls, and in our actions.

If we think morally correctly and our actions are in the interests of people and nature, then we show how rich we are. I'll tell you a story that happened three years ago. My house is small and neat. I have a new neighbor. He appears to be well-off. Even after his settlement, he continued to throw trash in front of my door and speak negatively about me, despite not knowing me personally. To put it another way, he tried to damage my reputation, even though the village holds me in high regard. I treated them well, and they reciprocated in kind. The new neighbor didn't hesitate to say and do numerous new and varied negative things about me. One day, he placed a bucket of trash outside my door. I simply disposed of the trash, cleaned the bucket, and then filled it with juicy apples. I went to his door, knocked, and after he came out, I handed him the bucket and said, "Here you, neighbor, you can only give what you have it more." After hearing these words, the nobleman seemed impacted and continued riding his horse without further remark. Hans caught fish in a basket, took them out, and handed them to Max.

"I'll catch them, but if you're hungry, light a fire and eat on the way."

"My dear Hans, I appreciate the fish and your time. God bless you." Max got up and went on his way.

Inactivity doesn't make things better

Max gazed upon an elderly woman and a man residing in a small house with a back garden. A man and a woman stood on the porch and enjoyed the sunset—the sun and the scent of the flowers. He engaged them in conversation about the pleasant weather and the beauty of the flowers and inquired about a suitable place for him to stay overnight. They noticed that Max was well dressed, had a pleasant face, and spoke in a polite tone, so they invited him to stay at their house. They welcomed him into their home, served him some food, and then ate together. They asked Max, where he was from, and where he was going. Max asked them about life in the village. Max had the impression that the dog never stopped yelping. He made sounds like he was in pain.

"What about the dog? Why is it yelping like that?"

"He's all right," said the lady.

"The first is lying on a sharp-edged stone and skating off the pain. All the yard is for him."

"But why doesn't he just move if he's in pain?"

The old woman smiled, and the devil replied, "Well, because he's obviously in so much pain that he can yelp, but not so much pain to move him from there. You know, we humans sometimes do the same things. We yelp and complain about something that bothers us, but we don't do anything to fix it. We only take action when the situation becomes serious and we have no other options."

The owner said, "Stubbornness has no limits. He knows there's something in there that's killing him, but he goes there anyway. Humans and dogs make the same mistakes, but we don't learn to adapt to changing circumstances. I understand that we feel uncomfortable in that situation, but the changes frighten us. We endure pain and malaise, often for years. Despite our efforts to relocate him, he continues to return to the same location. Like people, you tell someone, "Change the situation in yourself or find a new job that you like," but they don't do anything and only yell. So, our dog is like them."

"You're probably right," concluded Max.

Ignorance is a barrier for achieving happiness and success

 Max also observed the nearby village, which was in close proximity to the castle of the neighboring kingdom. As he was walking through it, he noticed that there was one person up on the ridge, and he was drawing on canvas. He went straight to him. He walked over to the drawing man. He completed a beautiful landscape on his canvas, depicting a child running in the wild in front of a lake.

"Hi. Can I take a seat, relax, and watch how you draw?" Max said.

"Sit down; I don't mind," the artist said.

Word by word, Max realized that the artist was a teacher. He painted pictures on a commission, even for the King's highnesses. Everyone loved and accepted his art as exquisite. As they were conversing, one of his graduates emerged, having completed a task his teacher had assigned him just a few days earlier. He had two paintings.

However, both paintings bore a striking resemblance to two drops of water.

"Master, I have fulfilled your wish. I did my best to hide their differences. Look at them and give your opinion on whether I succeeded."

The teacher answered him, "I've been teaching you for three years. It's time to teach you one last lesson. I think you're doing a fantastic job as an artist. Every artist or craftsman faces significant challenges in gaining immediate recognition for their work and, consequently, for themselves. It requires a significant amount of effort and perseverance. Very often people give up because they are not immediately evaluated and destroy their lives. I want those two of your paintings to be evaluated by the people here. I want you to go to the palace and place the paintings in the busiest part of the market. Place one of them at the beginning of the market, and the other one somewhere in the middle. Place a red pencil and a note at the first location, and instruct people to mark out things they dislike. Once you reach the second location, leave your brushes and paints there, and instruct people to make corrections to the things they dislike in a note. You will spend an hour strolling around the market, after which you will collect the paintings and return to me."

Max was watching the teacher, how confidently he drew, and how the brush danced in his hand. Time seemed to have passed as they engaged in a conversation. The student showed two paintings; one made him cry, while the other made him smile. Red crosses nearly engulfed one painting, evoking a sense of sadness in him. The picture, which he had poured his heart and soul into, resembled red eyes. He looked at it, feeling sad and resentful. Upon observing the other one, he found immense joy in the fact that no one had touched the picture or used any brushes or paints. They remained silent for nearly a minute or two before the teacher spoke.

"Dear student, when you first saw the picture, you noticed that by giving people the opportunity to criticize, they became ruthless. People who have never painted before have come and scribbled on your artwork. Make sure that when you begin drawing for money, it will remain that way. Because you are unknown, they criticize you, regardless of their understanding of these matters. In the second scenario, you asked them to correct your mistakes and be happy. Being a building block requires knowledge and skills. This ignorance prevents others from daring to fix the painting. Being a master of your work requires knowledge. Those who lack knowledge about your work cannot appreciate it. Your job isn't permanent, and don't argue with the ignorant! I want to ask you one more favor. Take this ring now, my boy."

He took the ring with the beautiful stone on it from his finger and gave it to his pupil.

"Please return to the market square. Offer it at least to five sellers to buy, but don't sell it to them. Just remember who and how much they will offer you for it. Go to the jeweler and ask for a price. But don't sell it. After all, I want you to go to the jeweler, repeat what you did with the other, and then return as soon as possible!"

This time, the student returned more quickly, arriving within an hour. The teacher instructed him to sit down and retrieve his belongings.

"As soon as I arrived at the square, I began offering it to all stands; I also offered the ring to the merchants. They looked at it with interest, but they offered no more than two copper coins for the price. Your jeweler confirmed that the item was indeed silver, not gold, and could only provide three silver coins. When I visited the jeweler, he immediately began to examine it. He offered eighty-eight gold coins as payment."

"I suggested you a way to understand the real price of that ring. When you draw a picture, it's beneficial to consult with a few experts who can provide insight into the potential price, just as you did with the ring. If you make mistakes, others may not understand your work. These people understand and will buy your work if they like it. As you become famous, your work's price and reputation will rise.

You can't please every ignoramus. Do not pay attention or feel sad about that, and you will find happiness in life and the joy of working for yourself. I hope you understand that over the past three years, I have taught you how to draw. But today, I'm teaching you how to manage later in life, how to not underestimate your work, and how to reduce the price. Say hi to your parents, and I hope you'll visit me from time to time."

"Of course, master, I'm grateful for everything you've done for me, and I'll come see you sometimes."

The student left. Max wished the teacher good health and went to the nearest hotel.

Affection is a spark; love is the eternal flame

 The sun was setting, and Max had to find a shelter for tonight. He walked all day without meeting anyone, passed through almost two villages, but never entered. He noticed that some houses were beginning to appear on the horizon. He quickens his pace in search of a hotel to spend the night in. At the end of the village, a lovely house caught his eye, so he decided to inquire first. An elderly man was sitting on the bench in the yard. Max congratulated him and asked him where he could stay for the night. The old man went to the fence door and invited him to come in.

"My boy, there is no hotel in our village. If you want, you can come to my house; I'll give you food, and I will give you a bed for the night."

They were sitting on a bench, while a young man shouted his name at the door.

"Teacher Tanner, we want to talk to you."

He went to the front door and invited the young man, who called him by name. The man was not alone; his wife was with him.

"We need to talk to you about a very important matter that my husband and I wait to decide on any longer," the young man said. Tanner brought two chairs for the guests and kindly asked his wife to bring a glass of blueberry juice.

"Dear young family, I am listening to you. How can I help you?" said

Tanner in a low, calm voice.

"My wife and I got married two years ago. We got along well for the first few months. Then we started fighting a lot. We are unable to achieve harmony, and our disagreements are on the verge of dividing us. Even our neighbors notice that we shout too loudly. We inquired about the happiest family in the village, and everyone responded that ours was an example. Please tell us the family secret, what to do, and why this is so unbearable; we are making a big deal of everything and arguing."

"Come inside and be my guests for the dinner, just like Max, who is staying at home tonight."

They entered the room where the hostess was preparing the food. She immediately went to get glasses, but the husband brought the table and chairs.

"Thank you for your help," Tanner said to his wife for the glasses.

"And I thank you for your help from the table and chairs," the hostess replied.

"Irene, tonight we have a guest who is going to have dinner and sleep with us, and we must prepare the bed for, and this young family is our guests only for dinner. Please prepare your favorite sweets for them to sample."

"Thank you, Tanner, for a pleasant evening."

And she started making the cookies. Tanner put all the dishes and spoons, pulled out the bread, and split. Bring a jug of water, prepare some more syrup for the guests, and then take a seat. At the time, Irene was still making cookies at the stove.

"Your young family should already be aware of each other's shortcomings. The key to family happiness is understanding each other. If you want respect, you also have to give it. You want joy; learn to make the other happy. Compromise plays a crucial role in maintaining a peaceful family life. Selfishness is detrimental for compatibility. Bad habits interfere with the harmony of understanding. If you help, you get help. In good times or bad, you must support each other. Constructive criticism is not an understatement; you should take a lesson. You must also respect the freedom of others. The truth is that you should not put barriers between you.

Everyone should take responsibility. Revenge will increase the gap between you. The pessimism will reduce your faith in the good. Forgiveness will fill the holes in your path. Insults will hurt you. Anger is the beginning of all problems. Shouting is an aggressive behavior that aims to impose someone else's will. The calm behavior is a balance for the person. Your trust will increase your hope. Hope will bring you faith. Faith will give you love. Your love will bring a smile, joy, and happiness. Everyone says life is hard, but you can strive to be pleasant, cheerful, hopeful, and useful in your own and others' lives."

Irene was ready with the sweets. She took a seat at the table and continued:

"This is how the world works: if you give, it will be given to you. Love is a crucial element that inspires two individuals to commit to a life together. The affiliation ignites the flame of love. But love is an eternal flame. If you love each other, nothing matters. It constantly shines and illuminates your path. You can overcome any unsafe or dangerous path by lighting it up. If a man only loves, he dedicates his entire being to making the other person happy. If she wishes to leave, he must let her go in order to make her happy, but he must continue to love her, always ready to make her stronger, regardless of the circumstances. However, if they both love each other, it will lead to a happy family life.

Love gives harmony and balance in the life of the family. Let's eat now." Everyone ate quietly. The young family finished eating and got up.

"Thank you both for your time and advice. We need to succeed because everything you've taught us comes free from the Creator, and you don't need a lot of money to buy a family's happiness."

"Thank you again and stay healthy," the young family said.

During this time, Irene gave them more candies. The door opened, the young woman expressed her gratitude once more, and they proceeded back to their home. Once they returned home, Tanner spoke to Irene.

"They both expressed gratitude, indicating a desire to progress together, and I hope they can resolve their differences. Now, let's prepare our guest with some bedding so he can rest comfortably. I think he'll be on his way early in the morning."

"Thank you for taking me into your home and feeding me. I hope you are always healthy and happy." Max said and went to bed.

If you want health, you need willpower and habits

It was a sunny day, and Max quickened his steps because he heard people shouting. As he emerged from the forest, he was greeted by a vast meadow teeming with people.

On another site, a large palace was visible. Many people were present in the meadow, watching and cheering on the competitors with their shouts. Some of them were running, others were shooting with a bow, and another was competing with horses; all of them were engaged in competition. With first sight, she was spotted off to the side of a small ridge to the left of the palace. An old man and a few children were standing on a small crest. Obviously, you can see everything that happens from there. He went there. As soon as he arrived at the tree, he congratulated the old man and the children before taking a seat next to him. He then gazed out over the meadow, where everyone was participating in their sports competition.

"On what occasion does this competition take place?" Max inquired.

"Some kingdoms engage in this practice when their kings wish to marry their daughters. However, the majority of the participants are nobles and the wealthy offspring of merchants. The winner receives the hand of the king's daughter. However, our kingdom has a tradition of holding it at the same time every year. Their involvement dates back to the era of this king's great-great-grandfather. They frequently participate, along with other princes from nearby kingdoms. There are always rewards for discipline. So, there is a final winner with the most victories in different races. As you can see, a large number of spectators and participants are present. It lasts for ten whole days. On the final day, in addition to the participants, the king also distributes free food to all his peasants, including those in his most distant villages."

"So, you have a good king," Max said.

"Of course, a person who does sports is always good with their own world view," the old man said.

Max responded, "Is only someone involved in sports a good person?"

"No, anyone can be good, but the one who is doing sports is definitely better than many others," the old man replied.

"Why do you think so? Could you respond to my question? I would be grateful to hear your thoughts." Max posed the question to the old man, curious about his perspective.

"When a person participates in sports, they demonstrate a strong commitment to their physical health. They make sure that their body is always in excellent shape. Therefore, he is not a lazy or cowardly person, but rather a man who struggles with courage and consistency. If a person is struggling to improve their achievements, they are putting energy into what they are striving for. When you have an aspiration, you are searching for a way to reach your ultimate goal. The person who is searching has the opportunity to achieve their goals. If he does not seek or set a goal to achieve, how will this happen? Like everything else in life, with the aspiration and ambition of a goal, with great effort, falling, becoming, and only the thought of reaching the goal, you will succeed. This person who does sports has a sporting grudge, and he spends it on training, and thus spends it on exerting his strength and not on other people. He burns his negative ego as energy for his powers. After he has burned the negative forces, he looks at the world in a more harmonious way and with respect for other people around them. By maintaining physical health, he also eliminates negative thoughts from his mind and adopts a more sober mindset, leading to a brighter and calmer soul. And chances of being a positive person increase. As you strive to become the best person, you become more equitable and less harmful to others. In our kingdom, there are individuals who live longer than those in all other kingdoms; even in the great kingdom, their numbers are not as high as they are here. Sport is a key factor in maintaining good health and a long life.

Everyone, if they establish a habit and possess willpower, can engage in exercise, primarily for their health and not as a reward. It's a matter of choice. I'm ninety-three years old, but I spend at least half an hour a day walking without stopping."

Max was quiet for a couple of seconds and then answered to the old man.

"Thank you for your response. I don't mean to sound condescending, but you don't appear to be older than sixty years old. Stay healthy, and I'll go over to see the riders."

Max walked towards the crowd to get a closer look. After passing by, Max considered participating, knowing that he had trained extensively and felt confident that he could potentially win in at least half of the disciplines. However, he recalled his father's request to document only the events, situations, and opinions he deemed constructive, avoiding any interference with arguments or problem-solving. He just needed to see. His patient's development began in childhood, and he possessed the necessary skills.

The lie is stronger at the moment, but the truth becomes stronger in the future

 Along the winding path, Max caught up a young man, who was walking slowly forward.

"Hey, why are you moving so slowly?" Max asked him.

"Hi, my name is Babekyan. There is a village before us, and there is a wise man with whom I would like to speak."

"Can I go with you? Your conversation might be interesting for me," said Max.

"I don't mind, because my problem is very big."

"If you want, you can tell me what is going on, and you'll feel better."

"You are right that when I tell you, I might feel better," said Babekyan. "I've had a tendency to cheat and lie since I was a kid, so I feel like I'm having fun. When I was a child, I lied, but the children forgive me. As I grew older, it became easier for people to avoid me due to my tendency to lie. I found it amusing, but once they grasped the truth, they became reluctant to engage in conversation with me.

A year ago, I was a shepherd in our village. They trusted me, and they gave me their sheep, the peasants, thinking that I would graze them all day, and I would not go to the village and serve the people, but would be on the pastures with the sheep. However, even there, I couldn't resist the temptation to awaken the entire village by falsely informing them that the wolves had attacked the herd. Everyone went to save their sheep. When they realized there was nothing to save, they returned and cautioned me, asking, "Is it really so difficult when you spot a wolf, then to come to the village and cry for help?" I was laughing, but they were angry that they left everything and ran away and lost a few hours of their time. In less than a week, I got bored and did the same thing: scare the whole village in the same way. I'm watching the whole village—some with kernels, some with axes—run back to the sheep. Since they weren't paying attention to me, the old man simply said, "Babekyan, don't play with fire; you can burn yourself." Repetition turns a lie into truth. Within a span of less than three days, a pack of wolves arrived and attacked the sheep. With all my strength, I screamed and ran to the center of the village, pleading for help, but no one even glanced at me. I believed I had rejoined the herd, but the wolves had already captured a dozen sheep. When I returned home in the evening, I discovered that our two sheep, five of the tax collectors' sheep, and three of the pub owner's sheep had disappeared. The village no longer wanted me to be a shepherd.

The tax collector and innkeeper agreed to settle my father's debt for the sheep, provided I left the village. So, I go from village to village and look for work. But in every village, I joked, and they cashed me. In the last village, I worked for the potter. But I stared, telling the other people that his hounds were passing water. People stopped buying from him, and the potter kicked me out. This is my destiny. I pray that the wise man will help me."

The conversation carried on until they finally spotted the village. They sped up the traffic to arrive as quickly as possible. Two men were coming out of the wise man's house. One of the men turned to Max and Babekayn and spoke.

"The wise man is alone; you can visit him."

They knocked on the door, and the sage appeared. He invited them inside and showed them where to sit.

"I'm listening, boys. What can I do for you?"

Babekyan turned to him and said, "I need help, and all he wanted was to accompany me here."

And he began to tell what had happened to him. Babekyan spent almost an hour telling his story. The wise man was silent, and obviously he was thinking about that.

After a few minutes, he finally started speaking.

"Usually, people lie when they want to achieve something in their own interests. If I'm not lying, there will be no truth. Every lie is valid for the moment, but sooner or later the truth comes out. Every truth is constructive, independent, and occasionally painful. Imagine yourself on a road, approaching an intersection. You ask a person sitting there to guide you to the village, but he leads you in the wrong direction. After you arrive in village B, you realize that you have been deceived, and you must return to another village again. You will not be able to recover your lost time. In a similar scenario, as a salesman, you were en route to village A with your goods, but you ended up in village B instead. Upon reaching the village, your goods suffered damage, forcing you to discard them. Not only did you lose valuable time, but the product you were supposed to sell to earn money for your family, which you would have used to buy food, was now lost. Imagine rushing to get medicine or help for your sick mother or child. They are doomed to die. You always put yourself on the side of the one who tells others where to go, but put yourself in the place of the one who will be deceived. Your father was hurt, and the potter and his family may sleep hungry tonight. That is the consequence of your action. If you don't learn your lesson, sooner or later on, you will pay for your sins. There are kingdoms where they cut tongues for lying. Since you've arrived here, I assume you've gained a basic understanding of what you're doing.

The lie fills the soul; the truth keeps it calm. Truth helps; lies hurt. The truth broadens your perspective, while a lie obscures it. The truth shows us the right way; the lie shows us the wrong way. Lying means losing wealth, but telling the truth increases it. There is nothing easier than telling the truth; to lie, you have to imagine it. With the truth, you can help; with a lie, you can kill. Truth is like a prickly flower; lies are like a beautiful grave. The hardest thing to believe is the truth; the easiest thing is to lie. What is the absolute truth, and I do not know. Come outside."

The wise man went out in the yard. He took a stick, scribbled the number 6 on the ground, and invited Babakayn to stand opposite him.

"Now tell me, Babakyan, what number do you see?"

"The number nine."—answered Babakyan.

"I see six. Therefore, I find it extremely challenging to accept your truth. How can I trust you when I see the evidence?

People often make the mistake of stating what they perceive from their perspective and accepting it as the truth, even though it may not be the correct one. Most of the time, the truth came out after the argument. But a smarter and reasonable way is to look at both sides and circumstances from all sides. But this does not mean that there is the exact and complete truth. But those people who can do it are closer to the truth than others because they have never thought about that.

Please think before you speak or act, then do or say it. Whether it is right, useful, or in helping a person without harming other people or harming nature. You can tell the truth or the facts. But whether this is true or false, it is difficult to change it. It is important not to harm yourself and others. That's what I know. That's what I'm telling you."

There were other people waiting at the door.

"Thank you, wiser man; I'll try not to remember your words," Babekyan said, and walked away.

Max left, too. On the way, Max turned to Babakyan and said, "The most important thing is not to harm yourself or others. That's the lesson the wise man imparted to you, Babekyan. I believe you have learned this lesson and will succeed and gain respect going forward. I wish you the best luck in life." Max went his own way.

Whatever you give, you'll get

 Max has already arrived in the village. It was almost nighttime, and he had to find a shelter. The village was devoid of the usual noise. The focus is on finding a place to sleep for the night. In every village, there was always a kindhearted family that gave him a shelter, and he always left them coins enough for the whole family for a month. He asked a child where the house of the grandfather, who always gives them treats without a reason. He showed him the old Michelle's house. Max knocked at the door.

"I am sorry, I'm looking for the grandfather, Michelle; the kids told me that he can help me. I'm looking for shelter for tonight."

"If you come with a good heart, please. Tell me, young man, what brings you here through our lands? Where you're from, where you're going, what you're looking for."

Max told him that he travels from kingdom to kingdom, from villages to villages, and describes the events and way of life of people who live there. The old man, pleased to see that Max could read and write at his age, foretold that Max's destiny would be to do good to people and to become a great man.

"If you have the knowledge, you are not afraid to overcome obstacles for yourself."

At the time, Michelle's wife was cooking dinner and listening to them.

"I'll tell you what happened in the village yesterday. We have a rich family. They own numerous animals on pasture, a large house in the village center, and the only store in the village. They had a son at your age. The father was an understanding man, but his wife called her a witch. She quarreled with everyone, behaved haughtily and mockingly, and was, one might say, the stingiest woman in the village. She raised her son as if he were a spoiler, showing no regard for others. A month ago, a beggar passed through the village, and he was repeating, "Whatever a person does, he does it to himself." And everyone who had the opportunity gave him something to eat. They even set up a hut for him by the river. However, after he remained there for a month, the evil woman became jealous and refused to give him anything. He teased her, and she decided to get rid of him. She prepared a loaf, laced it with poison, and patiently waited for him to cross the village, as he did each day. When she saw him, she called him, gave him the loaf, and said, "You are always shouting, "Whatever a person does, he does it to himself" That is why I made it for you.

Here's a pitcher with water for you, so you don't get stuck when you eat."

"Thank you, good woman. God will reward you for your kindness." He took the pitcher and left. He arrived at his hut and just started to eat when the son of the rich woman appeared. He was returning from his tour around shepherds. He saw that the beggar was about to eat and noticed the delicious loaf. He got down from his horse, took the loaf from the beggar without asking him, and began to eat. He said to him:

"You are a beggar; you receive gifts constantly and are accustomed to starvation."

"It is fine, boy. A good woman gave me this loaf. I'm going to ask again; you're young and you need strength."

He ate the whole loaf and went home. He was almost home when he felt a pain in his stomach. As soon as he got home, he lay down and squinted. His mother was happy to see him that he had already returned, but when she saw him squint, she asked:

"What's the matter with you, my boy?"

"I was fine before, but I ate the beggar's loaf. As I was passing by, I noticed a delicious loaf. It smelled so good that I immediately grabbed it and ate it without seeking permission."

The mother became hysterical when she found out what had happened. Her son was buried yesterday.

The mother doesn't know if she will come out of her hysteria. She is merely repeating the words of the beggar.

"Whatever a person does, he does it to himself."

So the beggar's words prove the truth that what we think is what it comes to us. When we say something, we think about it and make it real. People often say, "Don't judge; not to be judged." What you sow, you will reap. All you put on the table is what you're going to eat. Everything we give repeatedly, we will get. If we give poison, we will be poisoned. If we tell lies, they will also lie to us. If we hate them, they will hate us. If we rape them, they will rape us back. If we are greedy, we will drown in it. If we cheat, they'll cheat us. If we have confidence in ourselves, we will succeed. If we love, they will love us. If we help, they will help us. If we believe them, they will believe us. If we make someone happy, they will make us happy. Indeed, the Lord created us in this manner, my boy. Our thoughts are the beginning of our actions. Therefore, you should always think with positive intentions."

The hostess has served dinner, and everyone has begun to eat.

You want happiness; you must be sincere and grateful

 It was raining. Max was in a hurry to find a shelter. A large palace loomed before him. The palace gates were open. Max entered and immediately met two of the servants. They offered him one of the largest bedrooms.

Two other servants brought a large basin filled with warm water and asked Max to take a bath, as their king commanded.

One of the servants whispered to Max, "King Arthur greets anyone who enters our palace as a king, but sends them with a punishment."

No way back; he had already entered the yard; he needed at least to spend the night, and the morning he will think about that. They washed Max and gave him clean clothes. Max, with his manners, always gave thanks for almost everything. When they washed him, he thanked them. He also expressed his gratitude when they provided him with clean clothes. They served him royal dishes and royal food. Max thanked the servants for the king's generosity. The king himself was sitting on the place where Max could not see him, but he could hear him thanking the servants for their hospitality and for their help in making the place safe. When Max finished eating, the servants left and asked him one last time if he needed something.

"I'm thankful to you and your King for that you treated me well."

He lay down and fell to sleep. A royal breakfast awaited him when he awoke in the morning. He sat down to have a breakfast, and before he started eating, he said again, "I am grateful to the Lord that today I am alive again and continue my earthly journey. I am grateful for the greatness of the king; I am grateful to the person who prepared this meal; I am grateful to the servants who take care of me."

And he began to eat. King Arthur broke down and emerged from his hiding place. He sat down with Max, greeting him, and started eating. During their breakfast, they remained silent. While they were enjoying their breakfast, Max turned to King Arthur.

"Thank you for your hospitality and for everything you've done for me, Your Highness."

"I'm so glad you were my guest, young man. I have lost faith in the notion that there are no longer people who express their gratitude and appreciation for our services. For the past ten years, I have consistently encountered visitors or people passing through my kingdom, yet they have never expressed gratitude.

Despite meeting them and providing them with food and shelter, I have not heard a single "good" word from them. There were people who tried to rob me after all this, and I started rewarding them with a beating after every hospitality. I came to understand that people often find it difficult to pronounce the words "good" and "sorry". I also questioned how someone who is ungrateful could possibly respect you. Gratitude is gratitude for all that Mother Nature has given us. Sincere gratitude is gratitude to the Creator. A person should make beneficial sacrifices for everything and everyone. We acknowledge that the Creator has created everything and everyone. We acknowledge the Creator's presence in everything and everywhere. We can lie to ourselves, but the Creator can't. Being grateful increases what the Creator gives us. Would we have these bodies without the Creator? Would we still be alive if the Creator had not created everything that sustains our existence? The one who is happy. You have a lot of good things. Despite your education, you are still a young man, not a wise one. I appreciate your company, and the Lord will welcome you wherever you go. I wish you to be healthy and successful in life. Go in peace and enjoy. Everyone who wasn't grateful is waiting for a stick or a slap. Everyone who was grateful is waiting for their happiness." He got up and went to his chambers. Two servants came with a full bag of food for the road and sent Max to the exit, which was near the big gate of the palace.

Our destiny is what we've planned and decided.

On the day of his eighteenth anniversary, Max found himself at the gates of the Great Kingdom. He was glad he's already here. He missed his parents and his sister.

As he continued along the paved street, he could see his father's magnificent castle, which was in front of him. His family appears to have already received the news that he will arrive at the palace shortly.

At the entrance, his little sister and his parents were waiting for him. They hugged and kissed him and led him through the corridors to the throne room. Max asked permission to go to the bathroom first, take a shower, and change his clothes. During this time, the servants prepared a rich table only for the royal family. When Max returned, his parents and his little sister were waiting for him on the rich table. He sat down, and everyone started eating.

While they were eating, the King turned to Max and said, "Stay with your mom and sister all day. Spend all the day together. I'll join you tonight. However, we will postpone all engagements tomorrow and begin our series of note reviews early in the morning."

He left the king's dining room and went to do his business. The day was passing very fast. Max kissed his baby sister and talked with his mother. They prepared a surprise for Max in the evening, inviting his teachers and several young people involved in his education to the table.

The etiquette was to keep everything reserved and normal; almost all the time, they were asking him about things; from Max's journey, only the King knew about it and allowed himself to say some jokes during dinner. Everyone congratulated Max on his successful return and his birthday. They packed the gifts, leaving Max to guess what was inside.

It was a beautiful evening for Max. He was back in his home with his loved ones. The King wished a peaceful night and went to his chambers. Max's thoughts were flowing from one wise man to another. He knew what he had learned and seen for a year. He knew that tomorrow was also an important day for him. In the morning, he woke up, washed, dressed up, and went to breakfast with his family. He greeted his family and sat down to enjoy their breakfast. His father took him to the back of the king's garden to discuss his annual trip to other kingdoms after they finished eating.

"Tell me, my son, how was your trip? Are you happy, and what have you learned during this time?" the king asked with a fatherly voice.

"You told me it's a kingdom tradition, so I think you overcame this, Dad. I wrote three volumes of records. Some of these records hold significant personal value for me. There, I described things that are related to the daily lives of every person on this planet, and we encounter them every day. Others provide more detailed information on managing kingdoms, while the third section focuses on the benefits that our kingdom can reap. I will deliver them to our library, where I will select the ones that yield benefits, make necessary adjustments, and add a new one to the collection. I plan to revise and rewrite one of them, which I will then store under my bed. I need to read it frequently to ensure I don't forget it.

Because people are happy today, and tomorrow we will quickly forget what happened yesterday. Definitely, I had really learned from the best teachers; it is possible to be the best student, but the influence of the feeling is very strong. To control ourselves, we must constantly learn and not forget. I witnessed numerous positive aspects, but the majority of other kingdoms were plagued by extreme poverty and ignorance. I believe that ignorance and laziness serve as the foundation for everything. Not everyone can be smart or hard-working. But the people themselves do not have a normal upbringing and knowledge about a better life. It's not about that they don't want to; I suppose everyone wants it, but they don't have the conditions for it. Many kingdoms keep their people in poverty so that they can rule them easily. They are greedy, but they don't do anything to get rich. Many human kingdoms hold the belief that wealth is inherently harmful. I don't know if this is true, but our kingdom has no poor people, so the other kingdoms are doing it because they think being poor makes you happy. If you possess money, you are perceived as a thief, a fraud, or a tyrant. The truth is that being rich and doing something you enjoy is important; even being a stable boy is fine. The issue lies in the way people think—nothing more. Our ancestors built four buildings for the benefit of other kingdoms. My goal is to construct at least three more buildings—and potentially even more—for the benefit of the other kings. I want these buildings to be schools.

According to the wise men, other kingdoms don't want people to be smart. But I know how to change it."

"I apologize for interrupting you during your conversation, but how can you construct these buildings for schools? You understand that, as the King, I always consult with teachers, advisors, and merchants before making any decisions. After all, the people always have the final say. I can afford everything, but if I lose the trust of the people and the harmony is destroyed, you know that we will also become like other kingdoms," said the king.

"Dad, I didn't think that as a king's son, I could do whatever I wanted. I only express my opinion and how I see the future. I can't simply sit back and do nothing. I hope that when you talk about your motives, pros and cons, and if you prove what you are offering and I also receive your agreement, I will go from house to house to expose my intentions, and when I get everyone's agreement, then only can I work in this direction. We have our position, but the majority of kingdoms must align with us. In summary, dad, I am confident that the royal children will attend one of our two schools. Children from wealthy families will attend the other school. I think that I will be able to convince all of you and our people, both from the financial side and from the political side of that issue, because it is better to have a conversation with a smart person than a boor who does not like anything.

Therefore, our interest lies in their intelligence. You'll be surprised by how much they're willing to pay for education. My plan is to eventually establish a third school, for which we will be responsible for funding. Children in it will be from poor families. With permission, our emissaries will seek out talented children from other kingdoms. We will be the first to use their abilities, but in that way, they will also improve the conditions in their kingdoms. If we provide the right training to the sons of kings and merchants, we will gradually gain more and more allies. I assume that those who are against us internally won't have much choice as long as we are the center of all kingdoms. Through what they have learned, they can become more humanist and work alone to improve the way of life in their kingdoms. It all hinges on the lessons we impart. If we place a strong emphasis on the connection between trading and humanity, it will not only pique their interest in the trade but also leave them with a deeper understanding of humanity.

"You know, son, most of the wise men you've met or heard of are part of our people. They like you, volunteered after their last adventure, and decided to go live on other kingdoms and help people there. They chose their own way of life, thinking that they were doing something useful. I think that they helped a lot of people. Over the years, they have not forgotten us, and in many instances, we have sent them money to assist a family facing significant challenges. We have connections with them.

But your method is something else. You aim them lined up, so you spend money to make them look smart and human. I am confident that offering them money for their training will not be accepted. You have a fantastic idea. To achieve it, you will need a lot of help by creating the messages that you need to send to other people."

"I understood that if I like what I am doing, my life will not be boring, and I can improve people's lifestyles, and actually that is something noble. And if I have achieved something significant, it remains after me. And because of the good manners you instilled in me, I am motivated to help others cultivate the same virtues, as they are the foundation of all human problems. Ignorance creates fear and hinders success, and laziness prevents people from achievements. If people have knowledge and good habits, they will always succeed, and they will be happy. I am planning to devote more time to that initiative. Of course, dad, only if you let me do it."

"I personally don't have anything against what you think; everyone should fight for what they think is right and in favor of others. However, you must first spend a month or two preparing your arguments and motivations to persuade the initial advisers and teachers. If you can persuade them of the initiative's validity and its benefits while also demonstrating that it won't harm our kingdom, the likelihood of success will rise.

Anyone who backs you will provide unwavering support and assistance. However, I suggest you pause for a month before revealing your intentions. In the meantime, help librarians to record your notes properly in our treasury. I am glad you returned home safely and achieved your goal. Sometimes it becomes more difficult, but with perseverance and diligence, I hope that you will succeed."

The wealth of the great kingdom

How Prince Max's dream came true. He achieves his objective by acting and thinking appropriately. His approach makes it possible for a lot of people who don't have money to act like him and achieve their goals. Even now, this path is still followed. Max meets Princess Mary, the love of his life, while he is confidently en route to the destination. He believes that when we make use of our true wealth, life will provide us with what we desire.

MIX

Papier | Fördert
gute Waldnutzung

FSC® C083411

Zeitfracht Medien GmbH
Ferdinand-Jühlke-Straße 7
99095 Erfurt, Deutschland
produktsicherheit@kolibri360.de